The Phoenix Awakens

Koi Nikole, M. A.

A Virtue Exchange Book

Published by Virtue Exchange, LLC

Copyright © 2016 Koi Nikole, M. A.

Sharron Nicole, M. A.

Printed in the United States of America

Photos and Graphics by Michelle Lewis

http://ArousedByArt.com

Interior & Cover Design by Sharron Nicole, M. A.

http://VirtueExchange.com & http://KoiNikole.com

Cover Creation by Michael Bollenbach

All rights reserved. No part of this book may be reproduced in any form or by any means without the prior written consent of the Publisher excepting brief quotes used in reviews.

Printed in the United States of America

ISBN: 0692737154
ISBN-13: 978-0-692-73715-6

This book is a combination of facts about Koi Nikole's life and certain embellishments told from the author's vantage point and recollection. Names, dates, places, events, and details have been changed, invented, and shared for literary effect. The reader should not consider this book anything other than a work of literature.

The Phoenix Awakens

Koi Nikole, M. A.

DEDICATION

This book is dedicated to my children
Israel, Zion, Immanuel, Judah, and Joseph

As I carried your little life within me,
Birthed you into this dimension,
Breathed your name
For the whole world to speak blessings over you,
Held your head and your body
Through every stage fought on your behalf,
And have happily been the hand that feeds you.

Your presence has made me
Push, think, grow, prune, achieve, care and be
The Phoenix Awakens

Thank you for all the times you let me tickle you, enjoyed my sugah love kisses, and your many questions and needs that keep me on my toes and striving for our best. You are my motivation to strive, not just for more, but to do the right things each time that we might have fruit that remain.

To my Grandmother I call Momma
Mrs. Eugene "Genie" B. Lester

I love you and miss you so much!!!!!
You would LOVE these little people I have!
Thank you for always being with me!

To Zelda Fanese
Look Mom, I did it!

Acknowledgments

I would like to thank the following
who have contributed to my campaign
to put a FREE copy of
The Phoenix Awakens by Koi Nikole, M. A.
in every Women's Center around the world!!

Julia Hamilton
Paul Gilbride
Donna Hilliard
Linda Hill
Thelma Hilliard
Zelda Johnson
Dorie Mack
Glenn Person
Joel T. Lester
Bam Suttle
Bruce Singletary, Phd

Thank you for believing in my mission!!!

CONTENTS

	From The Author	i
1 - Crying Out		1
	My Big Daddy	3
	My Isolation	5
	Listen to God	7
	Don't Stop No Show	8
2 - Bleeding		
	Love Me	13
	Not Kingly	15
	While Cutting Grass	16
	It Came to Me	18
	My Fault	20
3 – Reasoning		
	Protect Your Heart	25
	Good Girl Blues	27

4 - Peeking

    Sometimes You   31

    I, Samson   33

    Oh What A Price   36

5 – Birthing

    I Am Still A Mother   41

    Yemaya   43

    I Miss Her   47

    See Yourself   49

6 - Nurturing

    Little Light Of Mine   55

    Step Above Love   57

    IZIJJ Love   60

    To My Son   62

7 – Siren-ing

    We Need You   67

    The Rug   70

    Who Is Who Ain't   73

    Broken Hearted Friend   76

8 – Lifting

    Consciousness   81

    Vision-Less   84

    Fear Is A Mind Dream   87

    God Is A Verb   90

9 - Seeing

    This Whole New World   93

    To Try Love   95

    Petal Love   100

    Us Flying   101

    Why Wait   103

10 - Standing

    Where I'm At   107

    You Looking For Me?   109

    I Like The Way You Flow   114

    Hey New Girl   116

11 - Equipping

    I'm About To Equip You   121

    They Thought   123

    When I Didn't Know Myself   125

    Unbothered   129

12 - Positioning

    Walk Away   133

    Get The Wheel   135

    Take Time to Align   138

    Do It Time   140

13 - Rising

    I'm Back   144

    I'm A Parachute   146

    Good Life   150

    Bio   153

From the Author

 Please treasure this book with love. These are not just words that rhyme at times. These are pieces of my very essence and excerpts of my life that you are cradling.

 These are tears of ink out of the scrolls of my reasoning place. This is ME I am giving you! So please treat it special, as pieces extrapolated from my heart that you hold in your hands. Gift this masterpiece to someone who needs a friend to walk them through the process of strengthening for a better life.

 Thank you for purchasing this book though to me it is priceless. For the years of hardship, hurt, triumphs, therapy, learning, awakening, to awake you ... cost me so much.

 My heart had you in mind before this project ever began. I was trying to solve for you, for us, so that we can be inspired to walk in the light of our power. It is written that your Eye might be enlightened and your heart would be strengthened. I want you to know you are never alone.

Love Y'all!
Koi Nikole, M. A.

The Divine has always been inside you

yet limited by you.

You hear in your ears and feel this

in every fiber of your DNA.

Divinity's purpose is beyond the dance.

It is to manifest. Now ... Create And Elevate

– Sharron Nicole, M. A

Crying Out

Koi Nikole, M. A.

The Phoenix Awakens

My Big Daddy

I was just going to walk out the door

Kind of, just float out the door

No drugs or alcohol just numb from it all

Just wanted to stop it all

I would have floated out the door, not worried about my children's future, needs, not even where I would go or eat

Just leave ... Just walk out and keep going

I put my babies down for nap and I went to the kitchen to clean

I cried as I leaned over the stove and I told Him

"This is not an honorable life! I would never want any of my children to live this way! I would not tell anyone to live this life!"

I remember saying, "YOU don't love me!! This hurts too bad for YOU to love me!! If this is love, I don't want YOU to love me!! I don't want it! I believed in YOU!

I started to clean and ... just melted down the front of the stove onto the floor

Crying, I sat there venting ... asking Him and telling Him

Then He said, "I didn't want that for you ..."

My big eyes peered over my tears ... like ... "Huh??"

He had my attention ...

He always spoke to me but this time it was different

He would usually gently coach me. Today He was pleading with me

He said, "I love you! I didn't want that for you. You asked me for strength and I gave it to you.

This was true. I don't remember asking Him for anything else. I was just trying to survive."

My raging waters were settling now

Calming into a flow ... much like a river

The Master Surgeon was doing open heart surgery on me on the dirty kitchen floor

He said, "I love you so much. I did what you asked Me to do."

His comfort just massaged my heart ... and my soul

I told Him, "What will my children in the children's ministry think of me if I didn't make it work? I wouldn't be worthy of leadership. What would my pastor think because 50% of marriages fail?

Mind you, I never asked how this life affected my children to this point.

He said, "You will talk with the Pastor. And if your God is his God, he will say what I am saying"

I, not at my request, gained an audience with the pastor. And sho' 'nuff, He did just that!

That was the beginning of the renewal of self and a new adventure of love with Big Daddy

It is in these places no one sees, no one hears you, and no one understands your road ... that Love heals.

So if you ever hear me say,

"I could grab Big Daddy by His ears and kiss Him in His mouth"

It is because Love transcends and love is to the core ... And He is mine ..."

The Phoenix Awakens

My Isolation

I've felt the pain of isolation

Your thoughts and looks of degradation

While I strive to stay noble, true, sometimes safe

Your body language and words say disgrace

See I have nowhere to go or run to

I have to be strong for me 'cuz I can't count on you

I know you say you love me, feels like a lie

I'm hurting and I can't tell you, I could die

This isolation feels like suffocation

I wish this manipulation could be my liberation

I can't really vent 'cuz you think you know the answers

Answering problems no one has, your attitude is my cancer

You don't even know who you're dealing with, you're fooled like the rest

Your advice isn't accurate, no clue of what's best

Not knowing the problem, you can't have a prescription

That's why it never works 'cuz you really don't listen

I'm not even the problem don't keep trying to fix me

I take care of everything, all the needs of this 6 see

Tired of talking about it, no one asked me what I need

To confide, to feel protected, for support, & love indeed

Koi Nikole, M. A.

I guess it's easier to hound me because you don't care about change

See you sleep at night, with your little good deed on your brain

Not making change, not helping us escape

Not strengthening me, running your mouth all day

I asked for a place to lay our heads, no more

You said I don't want to wake up to y'all on my floor

But you have no clue why I do what I do

His oppression and control sound just like you

I needed someone to sit down and listen

To hear my heart, help me, give me some wisdom

Don't tell me how to fix someone I can't

Then blame me for what he is or it ain't

When I reached out the blame from the lies hurt

I'll try to cover my kids and take it 'cuz reaching out don't work

Told look pretty, sex, cook good, and more respect

Jumped through hoops, anointed shoes, 14 yrs no change yet

Living their life any way they wanted

Laced with other's words, their expectations haunted

You care what it looks like and I'm standing here bleeding

I'm isolated, I don't need scolding, I need healing

So don't be mad when I purposely don't hear your words

Because I heard and felt life from another little bird

I pray you change from self to love,
And don't drive another into even more isolation

The Phoenix Awakens

Listen To God

--Only listen to God ... yet only hear me
--What is wrong? Just use faith to set you free?
But drag you down for your whack decision to stay
Same cycle you need saving again, just different day
Only to find what you were doing wrong
Was listening to them, confusion prolongs
Information dropped in your lap saying "run",
Intuition blaring the time has come
Your feelings are throwing up red flags everywhere
You're conditioned to say, "That's the devil! Beware!"
They press down those who want to be right
Their perfectionism makes them contrite
While the others get the applause for another deliverance again
Broken trails in the wings of their decisions
See it's the Price is Right, Come on down
Fame and glamour for acting like a clown
Miss Goody 2 Shoes, they say for trying to be right
Not concerned about how I'll be alone tonight
But I'm married
And the preacher on the stage at church
Telling me to believe God for the hurt
What if I choose to heed Divine Love inside
I better try to listen to God in me

Koi Nikole, M. A.

Don't Stop No Show

My goal is to tell my story

I will give my oppressors no glory

But I will tell of devices they used

Of their distorted ways and minds confused

Had me ready to cut off my life

Kept stabbing me and did it all without a knife

Give them no fame so you don't forget

Because there will be another that thinks they can do that

Don't take it personally when they come after you

Just move to the side and let 'em pass through

And when you don't react they'll bring more drama

Coworkers, children, spouses, daddies, and even mommas

You'd better remember you ain't a citizen in their circus

And only if we allow can their exploits work us

So understand how they operate and deal from afar

Because they work so hard to remove the strength of your star

So I'm transferring glory and power from the aforementioned

Uncovering eyes so you'll see their intention

And they will always know the right thing to do

But to them you have no value so they'll be uncouth

The Phoenix Awakens

So I'm here to tell you, You Got THIS!

Even if you think not, you can actually rock this!

You can walk on water and fly with your wings

Because you are taking full power of your reality

And when you smell that mess you gotta go

Because don't no monkey stop no show!!!

Koi Nikole, M. A.

Eyes open in the womb.

The struggle arrives to turn darkness into light.

Dangling on the wings of the Phoenix.

The creative process begins to turn ugly.

– Umar Bin Hassan

Bleeding

Koi Nikole, M. A.

The Phoenix Awakens

Love Me

I'm writing this lying in my bed face wet

My satin cloth pools my tears as I fetal on this bed

Pillow catching tears that won't seem to slack

I hate this feeling but I guess I'm back

Pulling my cover near as the Most High comforts me

While my heart feeling Love Don't Love Nobody

But I know it's not true because Love heals with no fear

But every time I've ever come to this place, You have always been here

Every time I've cried those tears You have massaged my heart

Upheld me with Your right hand when I want to fall apart

Sometimes you hold my heart up, So that it's not so heavy in my chest

You kiss my forehead, hold my hand, and give my mind rest

My mind keeps playing every incident where exactly he stabbed

I'm so drained from living & fighting I can't even jab

When he wants to do "him" You are always beside me to "do me"

Thank You in the midnight hour when & where it's so lonely

It doesn't really matter what I can't believe

It is what it is and now I'm grieved

Reliving the sadness in me today

Wishing all my hurt would instantly wash away

Feels like my arms don't have the strength to put on my shoes

Then I melt in my body when I rethink the news

And when I rise from the bed all of my strength is still lying there

Trying to make such a big deal in my mind into a small care

Being beaten down by blows of hate disguised as love

Or maybe it's hurt but I'm telling you it hurts, all I'm thinking of

Koi Nikole, M. A.

Just don't say anything to me or I just might start pouring

Out emotion as a pin to a balloon out of the sphere flowing

Just don't say anything please and all I'll do is smile

Because I have to get through work and children without breaking down

Thank you for being here with me, I hate coming together like this

But I am glad We're together, good and bad so this ain't just it!

Through it all, it's getting easier to see

I need actions not words and not potential but reality

Yes I love hard, am loyal, and with proof not just potential

Because my love is Divine and my commitment is intentional

You made me this way and to love this way for me is free

I just have to find that him that will love, like this, ME

The Phoenix Awakens

Not Kingly

When the motivation of your heart

Falls off your lips

And I nod, "Yes, King. I believe you."

But your actions contradicted

Your lips or maybe

Your actions were the motivation

Of your heart

Your lips, those liars, just lied AGAIN

Now I'm questioning everything

Motivation, lips, and actions

Having a hard time believing anything

You did, gon' do, infractions

 Thought your actions did what your lips said

Disappointed cuz' now my trust is dead

Just do what you said

With your heart right towards me

But your lips just spoke to me

You are not THAT Kingly

Thank you! *Waving & smiling

You saved my heart
I really needed to know THAT!

Koi Nikole, M. A.

While Cutting Grass

Sometimes you are committed

To love someone

And they are so committed

To loving themselves

That you get caught under the blade

Of their daily mowing.

I know from experience ... THAT HURTS!

As you try to fuse the muscles, arteries, valves, etc.

Back together ...

Huh, it hurts just to breathe.

That means ...

Be committed to love you!

Until you find one who wants to sculpt you

Instead of one just interested

In mowing your lawn.

The Phoenix Awakens

Koi Nikole, M. A.

It Came To Me

As long as the children have
Is what I used to say
Because I thought we were so limited
Few coming in so much to pay
I sang that for years before I realized
Not only was I not getting
But their lives were still deprived
I thought me doing without
Would bless my offspring
Instead it gave a mentality of our worth
And what family means
So while we were getting less
His action life was getting more
The drought was more than food
And my body was taking score
Children don't know what they should have
We don't have what we need but I don't mention
Because they didn't have it to begin with
So I'm giving my babies so much love and attention
But one day it came to me
And I wasn't even looking for it
Blinded by the care I was giving
And will repeatedly pay for it

The Phoenix Awakens

But this was a marriage
So my mind didn't understand
Why you wouldn't do your best
Or be a right doing man
But your actions don't change
Just because I finally see
The real you & what you think of us
It just came to me

Koi Nikole, M. A.

My Fault

---*This all your fault, God doesn't want this*
The text message read as my fears would insist
--- *You're doing this. So now I know whose heart is hard*
Said a woman I respected, no discernment, opinion now disregard
--- *That's what you get, yeah, acted like he was a king*
--- *You not sleeping here, these his kids, where's his family?*
--- *Mommy, you ruined everything! Why won't you go back?*
Ears noised, hearts poisoned as my heart I unpack
--- *Baby Girl, here's a room for your family, I took out my things*
--- *Thank you Daddy! I appreciate your love, just what I need*
Now I think about times I cried and pulled it together
For my church kids & friends, and at home for my children
Inconsistent on what I see vs. what I believe, soul contempt
Trying by the hour, powerless, but to do what's best for them
Riding in the backseat, friends trying to intervene on me
Family, one hand, Jesus on the other, trying to balance the anomaly
--- *You'll stay 112 lbs. you won't gain until you leave*
--- *Don't make the children suffer, I got you, what you need*
Since you decided to take the responsibility on yourself
Responsibilities, huh, I'll be unavailable when you need my help
Because I'm going to punish you for years, for leaving my control
Violence with my words, planted in ears and provisions I'll withhold
Even though it's for them, whenever your mouth ask
I'll play games, refrain, but parade them like I have

The Phoenix Awakens

--- God loves his daughters, I apologize you went through this
--- This was a gross perversion, it's time to cease and desist
So why do they keep pointing fingers at me?
I'm the one who makes shiny all that they see
Years trying to keep the wreck from colliding but I never could
I thought prayers and holy oil would do some good
What about me and mine needing a place to stay 2 months
While happy go lucky, lucky and happy, enjoy night life punch
So with all the voices, fears, and cognitive dissonance
I just wanted to be understood, my actions didn't lead to this
To this dysfunction that needed to dismantle to live
Side by side on a roller coaster ride with a heart that wouldn't yield
This is a monument over years, daily growing strong
Was erected and shaped way before I even came along
I guess this is where they say you can't change anybody
Just wanted to change how you acted to and about me
It wasn't my fault when she was your choice
It wasn't my fault when you wouldn't connect your heart
It wasn't my fault because I gave you another chance
In hope hoping my forgiveness delivered a better man
But now I know that I can't silence demons for people
Even if I give them ammunition and a platform to beat them
My fault was not yielding the red flags as they came
Sticking to guns pointed at me, BOOM ... is insane
I'll bear the fault and take the lick that I cut my noose
And how my misguided loyalty wouldn't let me loose
But I will not take guilt that doesn't belong to me
Because grown folks antics ain't my responsibility

Koi Nikole, M. A.

So I gracefully bow out from any interaction now as well
And I guess it is my fault that I refuse to remain in hell

My fault

Reasoning

Koi Nikole, M. A.

Protect Your Heart

I was that sister that believed in loyalty
True to my job, my God and my mate
God's way had always proven blessed
Until I met him
He was charming and probably too good to be true
I thought God said He is the one for you
But after marriage I soon realized
And these new antics open both my eyes
Drinking, clubbing, gone all time
Crying, begging why, anxiety now inclined
Asked me to stay home, thought that was a real man
Soon after is when it all started to hit the fan
One minute he loved me, the next he hated me
Barely home but in front of others wanted to date me
When it was good I thought it was answered prayer
When bad, I prayed he would care, though rare
Control my time, the finances and my feelings with your actions
Your blame and my perfectionism caused me many infractions
I was responsible for everything the smallest of fray
Withdrawing, withholding, flipping things I'd say
Sometimes I'd say, "Can you do it for the children"
But he loves the power of seeing me belittled
My fear was to not please God and not have His kind of home
That was an advantage and a ready tool for control

But God gives us feelings not to be suppressed
He's speaking through everything to make us get some help
When he made me aware, it changed my life
I understood my confusion, why I didn't think twice
Because my guards were down then it was way too late
Fear was there and too much on my plate
But the more I learned the stronger I became
That my bewilderment and my pain had a name
Breaking things, punching walls, and crazy out burst
Crazy enough to act a fool but not to physically hurt
It is to scare, to paralyze with internal scars
Make you second guess everything, those invisible bars
Eroding all parts of who I was
Just wanted relief, but I knew there was none
Prayer and sermons were my escape
No rest for the weary, these chains I could not break
Knowledge of this struggle & self-made me stronger
The power and control could grip me no longer
With experience, knowledge and wisdom, faith on high
Most High said you see that, now tell them bye bye
I was first transformed in my mind then my heart
Not perfect, but more in control of my part
Now I recognize, stop you in your tracks and don't think twice
Because out of the heart flows the issues of life
Knowledge is the power to
Protect your heart

The Phoenix Awakens

Good Girl Blues

I guess he thought if I wife her
Give her babies and offer a no corporate life for her
She would never leave and take what I dish
Work hard to be a godly wife and I run that -ish
And do my groove 'cuz she'll never leave
Got her locked for life based on what she believe

I guess I thought I was married to a man of faith
Time to move mountains and get this world saved
To stay at home to teach my children every day
Godly, pretty, wife, and mother, like the Bible say
So as you can see I never knew he thought that way

And he was probably sure this plan was fail safe
I never saw the change 'cuz it never changed at all
It was an evolving purpose, ideology set up to fall
But with all your intentions, you live one day at a time
So be sure each day you're pruning and watching your vines
I didn't think of what's best for me, that's Good Girl Blues
I never conceived my commitment would make me have to
I never knew I'd raise them by myself
From sun up to sun down always overworked
And continual opposition with no voice or say
Even though I do 95% of making this work every day

But I will never regret my little loves that came from me
But I know this is not what I thought it would be
But being a Good Girl, my intentions were right
Which has nothing to do with others on a plight

So when you deal with others please listen
And consider your capacity, in case love comes up missing
I know you trying to just be right
And you didn't anticipate the flight
Naive that everyone is like you
Honest, hardworking, committed and true
So you give too much, fix too much, and trust too much
But you otherwise excel so they don't think it's tough
But you hurt for the perfection you walk in
But stay a good girl because life comes back around again
Karma got your blessing and new walking shoes
Abundance if you learn how to overturn Good Girl Blues!

Peeking

Koi Nikole, M. A.

Sometimes You

Sometimes you believe in God and Love

Sometimes it's all that you're thinking of

Sometimes it's the wind beneath your wings

Because many times the wind is the only thing

Sometimes it dawns on you, you have to be your own hero

The counselor, fix it girl, mentor, and provider though

Sometimes the closest people do the daily stabbing

In the meantime you see it's at your table their grabbing

Sometimes you believe and work years with patience and sweat

Just to see them walk away is all you get

Sometimes you buy and bless, and to your surprise

You didn't do what they wanted this time

Sometimes they say you're mean because they can't get by

In time they get older look at life and see why

Sometimes you're the Mom and Dad, training day and night

Showing your daughters her worth and sons to love right

Sometimes you sit there wondering when it's all through

When most of the time your best is all you can do

Sometimes you set your mind free and do for you what's best

In those times walk away with no regrets

Koi Nikole, M. A.

Yes, sometimes you have to say what's best for me

Sometimes the choice is being bound vs. being free

Sometimes you have to separate responsibility from the core you

And let them process their hang ups out of your view

And don't take it personally because their brain's interrupted

Because 2 or more lives don't really need to be corrupted

Sometimes you must believe in Divine, Love Life, and Self

Sometimes within lies your protection, your wisdom, and your health

I, Samson

All of the levels of skill

I feel like wasted potential like Samson

But God, I thought, I was making God choices

Still wasted potential

My skills could have taken me so far

Chosen, gifted, and still feeling like Samson

Like Samson, I allowed my weakness to usurp what made me strong

Optimism can be a great motivator and a missed bull's-eye for a misjudged arrow

Loyalty, optimism, and at all cost faith

I was subdued, really clipped and repeatedly betrayed

But as Samson, they counted me out

Thought I was chained in the dungeon forever to not

Like Samson, I actually grew stronger in that place they destined me to

I was able to re-channel my loyalty, love, and faith to me from you

It was no longer trying to hold on to the dead

I had to rewrite the ideals in my head

My arrows have been getting closer but I won't boast

Just cutting out my captors, who spur problems the most

And like Samson I needed to let Delilah go

She was them and they like piety and church clothes

Like Samson they believe their ways which is their God

Has brought me to an abased position with smiles they nod

Koi Nikole, M. A.

They stripped and degraded loving my breaking

I'm an infused sister of Glory so prepare for my Awakening

Like Samson I'll entertain you my shine will blame you

You put in a lot of work but my ways gon' shame you

Like Samson I am a testimony to my mistake

Tell you with all things ... Stay Awake ... Stay Awake

Oh Sovereign give me strength to plunder revenge on my enemies

To take my experience, build sisters and brothers, tell them to go free

The dark place makes you think, re-enact, analyze and solidify

All the things that you can't do when the enemy attacks from all sides

Relief from the oppressors of the mind and body

Glistening, strength, built up, knowledgeable and shining

Braced these pillars one on left and right

Tearing down temples, against me and mine, with all my might

To disarm the powers, obliterate the towers, incontestable

My triumphant parade at the charade made them a public spectacle

The Phoenix Awakens

Koi Nikole, M. A.

Oh What A Price

<u>To My Past ...</u>

Now it took me a minute to think on this poetic op

Because though I release the pain for me, memories don't stop

But that's another lesson I learned over time

To pull down strongholds, palms up, get control of my mind

A lot of things were contingent on misplaced values & relational instability

So I had to build a wall to repair my soul and give contingencies for entry

And with all the begging, scraping, and trying to make due

I learned that my happiness nor provision could depend on you

And with all I was accomplishing it seemed nothing was ever completed

So I learned to think from all sides, bear the weight, and look undefeated

When you leave a strong woman to fend for her family or you're gone all the time

On-the-job training emotional & physical preservation, your place you just declined

So I thank you for strengthening my mind, heart, and my determination for provision

Catapulted my spirituality, unleashed me, and spun off my vision

<u>To My Present ...</u>

I wore your love like a flower in my hair, you made a dull world so colorful

You swaddled and revived me with protective love and I thought you were wonderful

The Phoenix Awakens

Infusing my heart and mind making my whole self feel safe
Reminding me of your imprint that could never be erased
Forming me, crafting beauty from your heart, arms, and hands
Melting my walls by calming my fears making alive like no other man
Sometimes I just needed to hear the rushing waters of your voice
Or our talks as we move about laughing at the world and it's noise
You peeled back layers and awoke things I never knew
And regardless of our ups and downs this healing honor belongs to you
Thank you that when I think of you my heart is still warm with smiles
Thank you for experiencing the love I gave returned back to me, reconciled

To My Future ...
You are the yearning of my heart from which my essence plead
But you've evolved as I've been in touch with who I am and what I need
I thought I needed one thing but I was able to see how superficial
A little trial and error, observation, & hope, all beneficial
I can't wait to bring my missing piece to your puzzle
And you surround my smoothed edges pressed in place, love snuggled
To form a foundation to build life, and impact the world and family
That the next generation & world will change because of you and me
And because you know your purpose, you will equip our children to last
Rising not tearing down, leaning on one another, I'll always have your back
But know sometimes you don't always know what you need
But we will discover best and be one another's retreat

Koi Nikole, M. A.

<u>To All of You ...</u>

So I garner the lessons that life has taken me through

I want to say thank you through the tears and smiles too

For all I've acquired, even my indecision prolonged

Because today I know a little better where you all belong

I have through you discovered who I am and don't want to be

And I've crossed things off, moved in direction to my created destiny

Because the School of Hard Knocks actually ascends in steps

And the more you learn and master, the more you elevate yourself

Un-tryingly with your actions you have built for me platforms to cross

And as I've shed insecurities and what they think of me, nothing was actually loss

I was just taking off, what I put on, to fit what you needed

So in return you cracked the shell and the true default "ME" proceeded

So I thank you whether you loved me to life or made me feel I died twice

Because now the worth of my diamonds are known to me,

Oh what a price!

The Phoenix Awakens

Birthing

Koi Nikole, M. A.

I Am Still A Mother

Motherhood has been
The most significant responsibility
I have undertaken mainly because
I have 5.
Whether I have been young or old,
With or without,
Married or divorced,
Employed or unemployed,
Housed or homeless,
With no assistance or no child support,
Loving God or just religious,
Knowledgeable or ignorant of,
On target or imperfect,
Strong or weak,
Hot or mild,
I am still a mother.

Regardless of our ups and downs,
The ebbs and flows of life,
If I have it or I don't,
I have to get it,
I am still a mother.

So from the inward parts
I have to suppress the hurt,
Shame, and pride.
Pull out strategy and ingenuity
And kneel with my hands open wide
In every area.
Children think it comes easy,
To orchestrate a total comeback
With only the clothes on your back.
I had to think about today, tomorrow, and next year
All at once.
Working 2 jobs at the same time,
Going to 2 different colleges at the same time
To solidify security
For priceless hearts

Koi Nikole, M. A.

Money can't buy.
The pride on their faces
When they saw me receive my degree.
I am determined to sit down
With my children for dinner
No matter what my schedule might be.
I am determined to have
Meaningful dialogue,
Provoke thought,
Orchestrate chores,
And direct their futures.
I banish fear
When I look into their eyes
And tell them it is going to be okay otherwise.
When I hold their hands
And pull them up as
I elevate us all.
As I carry them on my back
Across my own rivers of tears,
I am still a mother.
I don't receive pay for this job.
Most things I do work-wise
Are just to invest
Back into THIS endeavor.
I get paid in funny antics, hugs, kisses,
Good reports, chores,
And my own personal love
To make them laugh with my tickles.
I believe little lights of warm love
Are woven into my life as a mother.
No breaks!
I must pay attention
While keeping my eyes on each one's prize.

And so with the ups and downs,
The ebbs and flows of life,
If I have it or I don't,
I have to get it,
I am still a mother.
They are my motivation!
I heart all 5 of my Fabulous, Destined Little Loves!!!

The Phoenix Awakens

Yemaya

With Julia Hamilton in my heart

The woman that you love to oppress

Is the wife you should have with jewels dressed

Is the sister that nurtured you and had your back

Is the mother that gives life and keeps it all intact

We haven't seen her in history as anything but a slave

So we rape her into forced labor, braggin' and depraved

That here before us sits a magical goddess

Of all creation she is over and over genesis

She is deliverer and healer of sons, daughters, & grown men

She bears the sins, carries everyone's burdens & has the nerve to defend

If need be she will take her knowledge & equip her humble king

And his stealth form and equipped purpose will rule any army

And she is protected by his purpose and he is commence by her honor

To elevate him to ranks, her privilege and for this he loves her

For out of the womb, he became a recipient of life and he

From the love of the womb became a man now smarter than many

Because her head is full, adding, action-ing, transacting, all the time

Pulling down strongholds, raising standards, while juggling your life & mine

Koi Nikole, M. A.

Because her heart is full, she actively carries and multiplies the melanin

To raise mentally while you protect physically against forces to be reckoned with

And when we don't esteem the value of our Divine Way Making Queen

And participate in global genocide oppression to break her back and make her bleed

Then we blow out our own light and bite the hand that feeds us

Instead of harnessing the power of the only one who can breed us

For it is proven action that by her hand we are more advanced

Can you imagine? The world without her survival has no chance

We are protected by homes she builds and satisfied by food from her love

And protectively covered if she must, and taught to rise above

She infuses our lives from her empty tank that no one will fill

But they know she sprouts life's essence and they come to drink still

She is the fluid protection surrounding the unborn

Yet the refreshing drops and the crashing of waves for the forlorn

With her skirt in hand she moves to the rhythm of the waves

Gracefully with intensity revealing the power she displays

So instead of beating her down, restore her crown, because it really was gold

That she might teach things to develop kings for the jewels of her crown they stole

So let's harness the glory not blaspheme the ancestral taught sacred

And change the demolition-ing to building and polishing, that she might be elevated

The Phoenix Awakens

Because mahogany, caramel bronze kissed skin was never to be cursed

Her value oppressed too long, needed revealing and so worth is

Who can make a nation of any color, Mother of civilization?

So protect her as she nourishes you to prevent extermination

For all the hats, hurts, serving, saving, raising from this resurrection goddess

The closest thing to God is the Bronzed woman, just amazing how she does this

Koi Nikole, M. A.

I Miss Her

With Eugene "Genie" B. Lester, Climmie Harris, Thelma Hilliard, and Lavada Morgan in my heart

I love to sit at my grandmother's feet

And watch her eyes twinkle while listening to me

And I know I'm the fire in her veins

Her strength courses through me just the same

Because in her life she could see no other way

Married, young with children and mother said just stay

But every dream that sieved in her as a little girl

Seeing now that it's a great big world

So she whispers in my spirit, "Go for it and be free ..."

From every chain on the foot, heart, and neck of me

She's watched me as I've cried "I don't understand"

The years I lost trying to undergird a man

She wished she could have known to circumvent my pain

She felt with me the waste of years I abstained

Yet to hear my plans and humor on the other line

Reassuring my next quest and everything I learned this time

I'll achieve so she knows her being was not in vain

And ease the burden from which her prayers sprang

Koi Nikole, M. A.

So I wrap her in my arms and squeeze her tight

And her celestial kisses kiss me good night

Because I am the regal beauty, with heels, and a beaming smile

Swing waist like her and full of her style

Because time and space has no limits to our ancestors

So glad she's with me because I always miss her!

The Phoenix Awakens

See Yourself

We didn't see ourselves because we were taught

That our image was too dirty to possess glory,

 Wrong chromosome, wrong neighborhood, born wrong,

Been wrong since before we even came here.

Until one day your heart quickened from the pain

As the electrodes shocked your heart, somewhere between

Giving you a heart attack and making you breathe again.

And you cough the blockages to breathe life so necessary.

Gulping, gasping, grabbing, pulling up, waking up

From the bondage of cardiac arrest

Because I was obviously sleep

On auto pilot with an invisible yet visible pilot.

Guiding my will that I will obey

But nothing will work because it's skewed

And my independence prohibited relentlessly

Don't try it, Little Girl!

Koi Nikole, M. A.

Until I looked in the mirror ...

What the hell! Who was that woman?!?!

No light, no life, no will, only porcelain and a really bad job.

But the mirror showed me

What I needed to face looking at my face

In this place that sucked me dry and blew out my fire,

Or at least kept it low.

Looking in the mirror, I remember all that I was

All these things that were said,

Accomplishments that said more than people could ever.

My porcelain that immortalized me was now

My stone turning to flesh.

Because I possess the power of change.

To change, remain the same, create, and appropriate.

So by beholding my image,

I named, claimed, famed, or whatever they say.

I actually recognized the life flowing through me

And let what was in me nourish me.

The Phoenix Awakens

Feed me until I want for no more.

Never be afraid to look in the mirror.

You can't fix what you haven't faced.

And you can't soar without being convinced you can.

When who you really are comes in line with your mind,

Your Creator-ness will come in line with your actions

And will bring you to a place where you will love the mirror.

I love the mirror!

See Yourself!

Koi Nikole, M. A.

Life is in the globe I carry

for all those months.

I have been gateway to life for many

And a place of protection and nourishment for those

I have birthed in my Love.

I have held their hands and

Will carry them in my heart ... forever.

- Sharron Nicole, M. A.

Nurturing

Koi Nikole, M. A.

The Phoenix Awakens

Little Light of Mine

Thank you for making me stronger and gracing me with your presence

You have returned to the Most High where Love's world is infinite

No sorrows, troubles, or challenges on that side

No racism, sickness, or insecurities to hide

I cried because you were a part of me, bodily connected to mine

My thought for your future, anticipating your arrival and my new life

Of all the broken pieces, the times when I felt my body failed you

Losing my battle with faith, how my circumstances didn't allow you

To see your little heart pulse and think everything's alright

Too balled up, moaning with every turn, crying throughout the nights

I forgive those whose words were daggers that plunged

And bless those whose concerns and love soaked it up like a sponge

I still remember holding you, just you and me or just me

And comforting myself, dedicating you back to eternity

The Most High holding me together bearing up my cradled arm

In which you laid to rest, little with lilies, sweet and warm

Enjoy all the beauty of being with us but on that other side

Kiss our ancestors and tell them all I said HI

Koi Nikole, M. A.

I have grieved for the loss but have celebrated your release

Into the beauty of majesty and glory set you free

Thank you for warming my body and making me feel love

My every second reminder of what to live for

Making me imagine, think forward, and for bringing things to light

And thank you Most High for the supernatural grace & healing in the fight

For my mind, my body, my self-image, and my purpose

Yes I've tried several times, you have siblings though I was nervous

I know you're in the great cloud of witnesses, cheering us on

Knowing that our resilience and your love keeps us strong

Now that the tears have dried and sharp pains subside

And I have embraced your short presence in our lives

I want to love on everyone who has walked this path

And tell them the power of self-acceptance and love has

Your little sparks help me light so many

Thank you for being a part of me!

I release you!

This Little Light of Mine

The Phoenix Awakens

Step Above Love
With Willie Harris & Aunyia Monique in my heart

Sometimes, it's hard loving someone who you didn't birth

And even those you birth are not sure of your worth

And even though you have a role not clearly defined

Everything in your intent exclaims this person I accept as mine

Your role can add richness, more love, and reinforcing support

If no one feels threatened, understand the goal, and cooperation on one accord

But the person who steps above in love and shoulders those responsibilities

And choose to join, though may be severed, still commits endlessly

Because this is not a biological response but a choice they made

To try to give a child an intact home regardless of other choices displayed

You've thought long and hard to stand with the parent through this mission

You need the parent to back you up and be agreed in behavior decisions

And even though you accept, accepting you and your leadership might be a fight

Sometimes biological parents in one house don't support one another and get it right

Koi Nikole, M. A.

Remember, that's why you're there ...

So you, My Dear, must know your purpose and be clear

So ease up off the set and define what your role is and what you're willing to give

With the understanding of helping your mate bring a child a better life to live

And children change as time goes on so don't take it personal, unfold

But never forget the value, you are a gift and your added weight in gold

My Daddy once said God must really love you because you have so many daddies

Some withhold the bill, others eager to give which makes the Step Above a blessing

But life goes in a circle, I believe what you sow, you will reap

And if you keep adding the right things to soil, a harvest you will see

Though many times children don't remember until adulthood helping words and hugs

When you made them smile, gave your last while feeling unappreciated and unloved

Or you'll make your mate proud or the other parent may later thank you for your time

But more importantly you've invested virtue in your journey, the Universe always responds

So arm yourself with unconditional love and wisdom as any good parent does

Because your sacrifice is beyond the call of duty and it's a Step Above Love

The Phoenix Awakens

My Motivation, My Loves!

Koi Nikole, M. A.

IZIJJ Love

From the moment I felt you, you changed my life
Before any doctor knew or before I said a word, you were mine
You surprised me when you came with deliveries so unique
I loved your new baby smell, soft skin, and little toes and feet
But throughout the time I had many talks with the Divine
And He gave me the names to brand your life
Each of your birth had an individually purposed reason
Simultaneously going on in my life, a word in season
Your names were reminders of the promises given to me
And that's who I'm working to guide you to be
I named you, He proclaimed you, and brought you to my love
I sang to you, read to you and gave your back rubs
As I spread my fingers, smoothed my belly with the palm of my hand
Calming your soul, 'til you're in my arms or on my lap stand
I wanted the best for you, only Mommy's milk fed for you
Invested, poured into, providing, and fully protected you
You all are so different but add so much to my life
Your birth I would never change or think twice

Your name henceforth is ***Israel***
You have strived with God and man and prevailed
Hold strong until the Universe opens its hands
No one can stop the power of the seeds you plant
You are a reminder of the divine blessings of my course
That holding on will in due time have its rewards

From ***Zion*** which is the perfection of beauty
God shines forth, and shine she does truly
Through the rays in her melanin and loving heart
Her strength and intellect will take her far
A reminder the Most High won't be silent for me
In any situation Ra will rent darkness and set me free

The Phoenix Awakens

Told me I shall bear a son and his name called ***Immanuel***
And you will defy odds as I did naturally in birth due tell
That the Most High is always with you for what you need
To make you prosperous and carry word seeds
You are a reminder that I birth miracles within His Presence
That I am Divine, and the Most High is always with us

Now these 2 men are warring inside of me
Causing a risk, that health persist, requiring my safety
Protecting me, loving me inside out and didn't know
It doubled my tears, love, patience and mothering skills though

For ***Judah*** shall be on the neck of the enemy
The scepter nor staff shall depart his feet
A gentle lion cub but a passionate roaring when roused
And with his hands and heart he will lead those trodden down
Even as a part of me your hands were lifted in praise
To remind me to reach for Elevation in all my ways

Joseph is a fruitful vine wherever he goes
No matter what opposition, firm remains his bow
The Most High will help and bless from the limitless Universe
The crown of intellect and leadership accomplished in his works
You are my reminder that my path can't trump my righteous decisions
And nothing can stop my greatness and Divine vision

Israel .... Genesis 32:27-29
Zion .... Psalms 50:2-3a
Immanuel .... Isaiah 7:14
Judah .... Gen 25:23 & Genesis 49:8-12
Joseph .... Genesis 25:23 & Genesis 49:22-26

Koi Nikole, M. A.

To My Son

When I was thinking, "No!" Life was forming a "yes"

My body and emotions, your life seemed to possess

And I gained weight but I loss self

And put up with things I never would have

Because now my only thought was what you needed

My man child, juggle this and that to succeed and

Equip him to surpass every man I know

So I'd give him options and love to make it so

So I let him bang pots and play construction

Run with him in the yard and give him instruction

His essence still warms my heart no matter the ages

Even the teen years tries to rip out our pages

I want you to know I love you so much

Even ancestors will speak of the healing in my touch

And the way I can make a way out of no way

I cry out, call out, rearrange and save the day

To give you a chance I didn't know the world had

The best I knew how and all I have

The Phoenix Awakens

I did well for no one guiding me

Even though your young mind thinks I'm so mean

Because I've been your age and have seen this world

The choices that prove better and mistakes that swirl

And the regrets in life that delay progress

Because with these responsibilities, I'm delayed myself

So listen my son, ancient text says, "Pay attention!"

Mission missed & de-crowned position is your enemy's intention

So find refuge in my words and direction in my wisdom

To keep you from the streets drugged, dead or imprisoned

And even when you don't understand, trust my track record

To right you when wrong and for your good, direct you

Long enough for you to make for yourself wise choices

That pad your pockets, legally, and break all family curses

Trying to train you to be a man that we all respect

With the virtue of our ancestors guiding your step

So don't repel but let me mother you. We've already won!

Through highs and lows, I will forever love you, My Son

Koi Nikole, M. A.

"We are each other's harvest;

we are each other's business;

we are each other's magnitude and bond."

– Gwendolyn Brooks

The Phoenix Awakens

Siren-ing

Koi Nikole, M. A.

The Phoenix Awakens
We Need You

So do we feed the little boy jelly beans for breakfast?

Feeding grown men cupcakes, chips, and jolly ranchers won't help us

That decays the teeth, breaks down the organs and body

It starves the mind, that's what I see that surrounds me

When we ask for what is not relative to our health or needs

But we shout to the mountain tops and all over to be pleased

He put his hand in the cookie jar, a little taboo, a little forbidden

Because health and strength belongs to the wise, not to the malnutritioned

The more cookie or forbidden fruit, the more you think it's better for you

But it was never supposed to be for your good, just to show you, you

See when you know your role and how you fit in this dynasty

You won't lose focus and unity thinking what they can do for me

See you didn't know that your history and your present keep you numb

And you need the fire and determination of that special one

Whose struggle is yours for centuries, against losing all, defiant

She don't know what to do, she's trying to awake a sleeping giant

A sleeping kings, a sleeping healer, an ancestor for generations to come

Trying everything to make him take his place but he won't succumb

Koi Nikole, M. A.

To her passionate love, her proving her way

His eyes and heart are elsewhere, blinded by the distracted way

And we as a unified front suffers, so many holes and cracks

Because they are tending elsewhere, young men asking where Black men at

So they follow them marching, no skipping from our camps

While your African Queens are wailing, please African Kings come back!

But I'm not proposing African Queens be something else or for them to plead

I am calling for the heart of African King to come and fill our need

To return to the beauty you saw in your Mother, right?

To fix what is broken not to run from what you don't like

I know we're strong despite what I see

When I'm for you and you are for me

We live out a legacy, a dynasty, our history

You tending to our needs and covering me

And healing us from our past being a man I can respect

Washing me with your words, love and guidance

But I'm alone because you didn't know what you needed

The propaganda they fed you is what you heeded

The Phoenix Awakens

You felt you needed a trick to make you feel like a man

To keep you where you are and not rise to the occasion

No you needed your Queen like the ancestors you've seen

Making ways out of no way, breaking past boundaries

Your Queen is strong but together you are stronger

Tune out what they're brainwashing you, awake from your slumber

Ancestors are pleading for you to bring things back into alignment

Dominate, procreate, and orchestrate our divine assignment

Because when a man activates, though she had to wait

But triumphant is a family when its man awakes

I love you Strong African King, Love us Strong African Man

When our Kings say "I do & I will" Our family & community says "I CAN!"

Koi Nikole, M. A.

The Rug

It's not worth it
Too much of an investment of
Self, time, memories, heartache,
Re-heartbreak, picking up
Clearing up,
Getting back, and over thinking
To come to the place where
No one wins not even you

And she is going to give this guy some
And prove to him that she can do better
She's gonna hold those children tight
And pull them closer
If she perceives he's trying to hurt her again
But whether it is her hate that makes her
Snatch the children away
Or she just can't and won't
Take another stab from his knife

And he's going to give that girl some
And prove to her that he can love someone
Better than he did her
Since she wanted to leave
He's gonna show her

The Phoenix Awakens

And whether it is his hate
That makes him snatch money
Off his childrens' plate
He's not gonna let her win
Or make him do anything

So now she's stronger than ever
And the children are better
And she showed him she didn't need him
To pay for these children or raise these children
But she is overworked and over hurt
And never really able to love beyond
Proving the point
That she didn't go under
Despite having the rug pulled from under her

So now he's stronger than ever with his new family
And he showed her
How good of a husband and father he could be
But he's fathering another's children
That get more time & love
Than his own creations ever did
While proving the point
That he didn't go under
Despite having the rug pulled from under him

Koi Nikole, M. A.

The illusions of wins are losses

Lying there waiting under one's feet

Because the fact is

The children are starving and hurting

And so are you

So blinded by your hurt and trying to hurt

And no one wants to choose

What's best for the children

Despite having the rug pulled from under them

The Phoenix Awakens

Who Is Who Ain't

I hear men and even women say

It is the Women's fault the state of the man today

With all these single women leading these homes

I tell you, everything was bound to go wrong

Incarceration and femininity stripping their manhood

So how is that the fault of one trying to savor the good?

"You making punks out of these guys supposed to be men"

She's doing all she can only government pitching in

Female-led homes high, men don't know who they are

The mother is left with this mess & expected to raise the bar

If you did it right or wrong it doesn't even matter

It's you both so both make the solution happen

If she's dumb then you have to be dumb too

But you continue to be dumb, while she covers for you

It's not dumb women choosing dumb men that's all wrong

It's just brothers that won't stand up and be grown

Yeah I said that ... Brothers ...

Koi Nikole, M. A.

Every parent black and white stand at the fork on the journey

"Do I provide & train my kids or do I turn my back & do me?"

That pivotal place in the heart you arrive at every single day

For the mother there is no choice, her strength is made that way

Cultures that value the gift in women, their men lead their homes

Because the wealth of the family's gift is harnessed and honored as gold

But you break her down with your actions, rumors, and words that curse

You snatch their finances like "Nah", to make it even worse

Then ask the Judge man "Can I take more from my children's needs?"

He's paying his dues every day, he's like, "Joker, please!"

If you help a man dodge responsibility, you'll help him again

Because he never learns to raise himself so the cycle never ends

With no-help-dad, judges, peers, hip-hop, tv, and self

These are mothers only help, so what can you expect

She does everything she can to provide until he's on his own

To teach him the man, Jesus, and make him a moral soul

And they do a great job! Keep in mind, so much lacking

She's learning as she goes, she's doing good considering

The Universe is calling for you to be that Jesus

You've quieted the voice of your children saying "Daddy don't you need us"

The Phoenix Awakens

Well you do because it is the fulfillment of your purpose

The reason you were created and preserved, not to create a circus

So when you're tempted to blame her, brag for the things she does

Think twice because she is the picture of the true image of love

Go to brothers and ask them to do equally as much

And you will revolutionize your numbers with just that touch

Stop degrading mothers for giving their all

And applauding fathers for doing not much at all

At least encourage brother to invest equally vision, training, & money earned

So respect can grow and the next generation can learn

When you value the women, marriages and families are strong

Harness that value! It's the key to keeping it from going wrong

Be thankful for the woman serving humanity, making "can" out of "can't"

The problem is not the female who IS doing her job but WHO AIN'T!

Koi Nikole, M. A.

Broken Hearted Friend

Today I felt lonely and so confused

Even sadder at the fact I couldn't turn to you

But even when times are great and I have good news

A little sunken at no reply whenever I reach out to you

My subconscious dreams to compensate for the need unmet

Only as I slumber my heart visualizes the fun I don't get

I remember you walking smiling saying, "I hope that's not it"

But it feels like confusion blew out the fire, reality sometimes hit

I really needed you there, when I didn't know what to do

For some reason I'm connected and I know you need me too

It is almost like my soul is fused, there is no sequel

Because all friends planted in my life are not created equal

We used to feed off each other's creativity, a world our own

With intensity and even spirituality, unveiled in that zone

But to this day what I do, trying to stick won't stay

I believe your heart wants to tell me what your mouth won't say

I'm not sure what it is and at this point I really don't care

I just want to understand, be understood, and our connection repaired

The Phoenix Awakens

I believe you're pulling my heart strings for a divine purpose

Because the rejection is real, over and over, just gets worse and

So I love and hate, let go and try to wait, storm that won't settle

Changing dispositions, emotional tides, heart pushing water petals

Maybe it's more to me than it meant to you

Heard I'm loyal to a fault and that's sometimes true

But if I could just close my sincerity off and never feel again

It would actually be untrue to my nature and my heart as your friend

I do believe our cloud of witnesses keeps these strings intact

Because we yet see what they see and don't see what we lack

Maybe if we can both sit down, bear our hearts to turn it around

Accept the truths, learn how to relate, instead of hurt compound

I know you have friends you grow with, and I'm not right now one

And in your new endeavors and circles you're having so much fun

But my heart is missing my friend's love

And I want to tell you all I'm thinking of

And be my natural mess, creative self, bouncing off your vibe

Kickin' it, laughing, family, and music that don't stop

So I'm grieving today of a friendship love that went away

But the Most High can tell you, I miss you so much today!

Signed,
Your Broken Hearted Friend

Koi Nikole, M. A.

"The real power

behind whatever success I have now

was something I found within myself—

something that's in all of us, I think,

a little piece of God just waiting to be discovered."

- Tina Turner

The Phoenix Awakens

Lifting

Koi Nikole, M. A.

The Phoenix Awakens

Consciousness
With Tina Miller in my heart

The state of being awake and aware of one's surroundings

The amount of people sleep walking eyes open is astounding

I freakin' applaud consciousness and conscious people!

Because it is not sitting somewhere palatin' what they're feedin'

Whatever someone decides to regurgitate to you

And you parrot the same words not even thinking it through

Consciousness has no color but is the path to knowledge and freedom

Consciousness means to be awake from sleep, to be a critical thinker

It is about recognizing and cutting the strings of the puppet master

In the mirror, brain cleaned out, filling with truth thereafter

Consciousness is an awakening to the fact of what is internal and external

Realizing heaven can be right now on earth just as hell is a present inferno

It is about you having the key and simply unlocking the chains

That have you bound first in your mind, cognitive dissonance on the brain

It is a hunt, a quest, to capture, to right the wrongs

It is not being spoon fed but seeking out of your comfort zone

Koi Nikole, M. A.

Searching out truth because you are so hungry and milk no longer can satisfy

Idly standing outside yourself, watching yourself waste, and walk on by

It's about being called and thought of as whatever because you know there's more

They don't realize you know your truth and theirs, you're woke while they snore

You want to abolish all smoke screens and choke smoke screamers

With the false charisma called marketing that just keeps us dreamers

That we might gravitate to enlightened states of ancestral wisdom

Where we have no choice but to judge the futility of this system

And add strength through opening doors to a direct Divine access

While the processes that have middle men prove to be abscessed

How the world tries to keep sucking me away from my melanin fuse

While I lay in the dialysis of life, purified of life and so confused

How it keeps trying to feed me poison and pills and parades that kill … me

I just want us to wake up and go forth in who we're supposed to be

Not tied with water and sticks turning holy tricks

To obscure the light from our lives like an eclipse

The Phoenix Awakens

To wear the holy crowns of our ancestors in our hearts with every breath

And honor God in all creation, and preserve our world from death

To resurrect the family before evil, greed, and hate were put on our plates

And be holistically freed from needing remedies for diseases we intake

To raise Brother and Sisters accepting their own standards of beauty

And reinforcing the family unit, giving true life in family and community

But know the bases of Who God is, no eyes covered with sheep's wool

Transcends all gadgets and gimmicks that end up controlling and belly full

Be filled with recognizing His face, and feeling the pulse of His heartbeat

In understanding His desired end result and you will find peace

You won't be the same, you can't accept just anything anymore

Because the Lion is awakened, getting stronger, and the Most High wants you to ROAR!

Koi Nikole, M. A.

Vision- Less

Sometimes people are so focused & won't see the big picture

Don't know how to see forward their own future

And then they want to be all one with you though

You, with their vision, only so far you'll go

Don't care about investing or how that affects others

The consequences thereof because the future doesn't matter

With a blind man, you will go absolutely no where

He doesn't see a future so why should he care

His vision is only now and what he can in front see

If not instant gratification he will fall back and retreat

They will burn down the forest just to get a flicker

Or end up locked up for fake diamonds that glitter

They will chase waterfalls possessing nothing at all

Just to feel in pursuit, looking busy is his downfall

Just to say I did it my way

In the same place 5 years ago today

They will burn important bridges that hold them in mid air

But only after they cross them, so be aware

The Phoenix Awakens

The big picture is distorted and not clearly seen

For its wholeness, clarity, and the mission it brings

But he bases his decisions on a moment or his choice,

This opportunity or this gimmick or a smooth speaking voice

But it's this wife, these children, this life we've built

Our purpose together and where we're supposed to steer this ship

When you are not looking at or cannot see the big picture

You will soon not have the big picture with ya

It is not even in your ocular concept to uphold the vision

The connection of who you are in the future is missing

He cannot uphold, maintain, or even see the value in

What he cannot taste in heart is not a lasting decision

He can't see the reason to invest himself or at it work

And if you love him to death it's gon' hurt

So if he can see part and not whole

The part that he sees can only be his goal

The rest of the big picture will fade out of view

And only a small part of what he can see will belong to you

Koi Nikole, M. A.

But if he can see the big picture, embrace and protect

Then he can make a path and chart you all's next step

And not a part but the whole is now his own vision

It is more likely than not, the fullness will come to fruition

You cannot inhale the big picture focusing on a stroke

Following every scheme, ignorant of the system, ending up broke

Cannot live for the moment and have it all though

All is not even in the range of your scope

Should want family, wealth, health, lineage, and happiness

You gotta be feigning for it, and create the readiness

No strategic end in living moment to moment

Proven path & consistent action is the missing component

Requires discretion, balance, empathy, and counting cost

Do you see now how so much is lost?

Don't let the vision-less in, don't snooze

Because he's reckless, self-serving with nothing to lose

He cannot see his way

He's vision-less

The Phoenix Awakens

Fear Is A Mind Dream

I think my stomach hurts, I mean my heart or my head

My feelings, my viewpoint, my posture, my story unread

I'm dreaming, keep moving, trying to run away from

This scary dude paralyzing my body and soul when he comes

The big hand that wants to pause me with his paws see

And I just keep running trying to stay free

Each step at each turn I try to keep don't my anxiety

So I can think clearly where to run so he don't catch me

This shadow has no power over me, I'm sleep what can it do

So keep running 'til the sun comes up, I guess 'til it dawns on you

OMG He's right there but he's just a figment of my imagination

But he's at every turn, I feel his presence, about to put in my resignation

My fear of the unknown, scared and don't know what or who

The truth is it doesn't matter, it's not about them but about you

This is your state of unconscious revealing to you what's in your head

Trying to reconcile what being awake can't heal or take, so we're here instead

Some say fear is false evidence appearing real

But it's real, wake or sleep because of how it makes you feel

Koi Nikole, M. A.

See people are chained to invisible emotions all their life

So the power will take yours, suffocate, or give you life

So if I get the same feeling whether sleep or woke

What's the common factor overworking the scope

It is what we hold onto that cause us to be uneasy

What you feel you have power over don't make you queasy

And what if your mind knew you have power over everything

Then you would not have nightmares, they would all just be dreams

And they'd play like action movies, like when the antagonist combust

And your super powers transcends power, another one bites the dust

You feed your dreams the power it has

To make you levitate, eye power disintegrate or kick the enemies ass

Learn how to in your mind not to accept or take that fear

But through knowledge of self-power, make them fear coming here

No disrespect but your Deity cannot triumph the power your mind holds

But the mind brings to fruition the Deity's wishes to unfold

So when you learn to still and direct your mind, even unconsciously

You have harnessed a power to propel yourself, you see

The Phoenix Awakens

In fact be conscious be alert and aware even when you lie dormant

That your power is overcoming & the Most High is your endorsement

If you say you can you can, if you say you can't you can't

Take it from someone who always has a lot on her plate

Your thinker will ransom you and with its power you will not break

Now you have the vested ammunition for victory, even when you are awake

Koi Nikole, M. A.

God Is A Verb

He said what if God was also a verb ...
I replied He is but our thinking and the way we use words ...
Even the word "God" is our human intelligence trying to define
To contain microscopically for our study to propel or benign
But this force is not a man with a million jobs, hats, and accolades
We've reduced the creating energy so our rightness we can parade
Vitality, motion, movings, that's how we know He is in action
Not because we give him names for our conscience connection
We understand Divine presence has taken place when action occurs
And because of the way we view God we made a noun what was a verb
Healing, providing, protecting, revealing, loving, correcting, and being
When these actions happen we know the Divine is transacting
So let's be aware that whether we do or not it is happening
Whether you acknowledge, accept or stand erect, ways are functioning
It would behoove you to step into moving waters to revive
To stir up life instead of just surviving and empowering your Divine
Because when you are plugged into the Source, always current and on
Then your light of healing, providing, loving and relating is so strong
So by the power invested in you I command you to go and move see
A belly from hunger, heart from brokenness, chains of the mind to free
Because you are that utensil fashioned to feed the world
So don't limit the expanse with words, you are the tool of the Verb
So know God is a verb that ripples through life and makes you feel
Hairs standing with chills, stress dam just broke the Verb in action is real

The Phoenix Awakens

Seeing

Koi Nikole, M. A.

The Phoenix Awakens

This Whole New World

As I smoothed out the creases in my comforter and walked into the living room

Lit by the rays from the sun bouncing off the glass coffee table

As I soaked in the peaceful aura of the harvest, ancient, African décor

Peace rested in my soul

Aaaah ... yes

What I thought would be the end of the world

Had become a whole new world

All the fear of not knowing what would happen next

Or the oppressive feelings from the chaos and unalignment

Melted in me

Probably a while ago

So to culminate the thought, the ambiance, the visual

My tranquil movements, and my arrival

Ha! I've created a whole new world

Koi Nikole, M. A.

I am actually in the most poised place for the best

Which is yet to come

But the feeling of time standing still

Quiet serenity screaming

I love you for this moment with no agenda

But to the lake to take a break

To settle, to still, feel, and listen to create

To create more of

This whole new world

The Phoenix Awakens

To Try Love

When the earth opens whether it shakes, breaks, or quakes

Or you hand scoop to part the brown sea for newness to elevate

You have to be fallow, ready, and supple

Movable, willing to turnover, cover, and be covered

This seed here ain't no ordinary seed

It's destiny filled, pleasure giving, life long, and meeting needs

So keep your eyes open and words spoken be not forgotten

For that longing you feel at the core will touch you, just stay open

So let's communicate not fluctuate, just ride the tide

Commit to enjoy the good connections and take it all in stride

So I'm not asking you if you feel but telling you when you yield

To this flow, I feel the unthinkable, signed, delivered, yet sealed

I understand that the genius and fragile heart was not handled, but compromised

And though it hurt like hell, and felt like you would break, I apologize

That's not my purpose in your life nor my job, station, or post

It will mar the beauty that I am, that we are, and hurt us both

Koi Nikole, M. A.

I'm here to make you speechless by taking love down your throat, making you choke

Clutch your chest, resuscitate your heart, and kicked back blowing smoke

Two fingers at your lips holding a memory of what it felt like in your mind

Because it eased tension, did I mention, the world for a moment had to recline

You can't come at this like you've tried before

Anything you want is worth pursuing and fighting for

So let's eliminate the hide and seek

Being ourselves, no mask, so to speak

And for you to share without judgment openly

But in a discovery of who we are supposed to be

As we in life are discovering and uncovering

We are offering, watering, and coloring

Wondering, considering, and showering

Laboring, thundering, and yet towering

I want to uncover that hidden that might be in us

To add healing to our journey and learn again to trust

The Phoenix Awakens

I am your resting place, your shoulder-to-shoulder comrade

I come to shake up your normal, adventure and love to add

I'm not here to compete with you, I'm not your opponent

But to fertilize the beauty so needed for growing

To walk this road with intimacy and intensity

Explode from your mind, body, heart 'cuz you're so into me

Toes tingle, with my mingle that your mind is spilling out overflowing

Catching your breath, triumphantly with a smile on our face knowing

And I don't even have to touch you ...

Man, you know that's so smooth ...

Sometimes you need the dirt and just a desire

To create life, seeds, and beauty make worth transpire

Don't let your hesitation be procrastination and miss a great start

You may have to give up on your perfected illusion and follow your heart

Because this is between you and I not you and you, reset

We evolve and you don't know all that you need and love yet

So you don't justify, wait, preparing for something you may lose

Don't overthink what you don't know, go with what you know and choose

To Try Love

Koi Nikole, M. A.

The Phoenix Awakens

Koi Nikole, M. A.

Petal Love

As my cheek brushes the pillow
The warmth in my heart
Travels around my neck with a hug
And kisses my little brown nose
As I inhale the floral scent
That relaxes every limb
I collapse back onto the bed
And grab my pillow
Removing the rose petals
From my hair
My eyes land on a beautiful bouquet
Encapsulated in sparkle cut crystal
I feel love resonating all over
Because you know
I love these things
And that you desire
To make me feel
Your Love.

The Phoenix Awakens

Us Flying

I have no desire to be the stereotypical strong black woman.

My desire is to be The Woman

That is Queen with her King.

It is to walk hand in hand with my man

And imperatively he holds my hand

We're so progress the world

Has no choice but to,

on several levels, be blessed!

He's not only one with me

But he walks with me

He's fine with who I am

He will run with me

To or from ...

We will run so fast

We will fly together holding hands

Going from level to level

Glory to glory

Business, pleasure, relationally, family

Koi Nikole, M. A.

That's what I'm looking for

Nothing less

With our biological and spiritual children

Holding the end of our sashes

Flying with us

High

Above all the standards, levels, and mouths

Trying to keep us from going high permanently assembled

I want forever

Us flying...

The Phoenix Awakens

Why Wait

Beauty is in the eye of the beholder

I thought I failed the test

Yet while all are looking, only you saw me

My heart, my pain, my potential and willingness

At the window of my soul who takes the time to inquire within?

This seer, invader, is My Love, and now my best Friend

I was trying to find my place

And be discovered by Love

When I went left, it seemed to go right

This time I obviously went right because

I ran smack dab into you, My Love

Even though I carry these bags,

You were willing to unpack them

Rest me from my weary journey, and take what I have

Love makes you say I want to make this person only mine

And take them off the market, unavailable for all time

Koi Nikole, M. A.

I guess you came looking and I came to be seen

By your eyes, touched by your heart, touching my everything

I connect with you, I can trust you,

I believe you are a vital part of making me

For me to be the wind beneath your wings

And for you to bring out the best in me

Respect, commitment, and love is what it takes

To build a life together and you didn't hesitate!

So Divine bliss on all we come together and create!

I love that you're about action

Saying let's do this ... Why Wait!

The Phoenix Awakens

Standing

Koi Nikole, M. A.

The Phoenix Awakens

Where I'm At

After I have healed from the scars

After understanding love is right where you are

I had to understand what was really going on

What is it that I'm doing so wrong?

I had to connect how I'm wired a little better

And how the end known first really does matter

I'm learning everyday what hooks me and a little more why

But I understand how even if I fight, it still dies

It's like a flicker in the wind vs. a glowing fireplace

Gives light, warmth, cooks food, illuminates the whole place

Where the flicker, you can't see nothing 'cuz it keeps going out

Quick finish last a minute not meant to be a functioning light

So many different kinds of love all with a different purpose

These people aren't your enemy, your detection just ain't workin'

We see pretty faces in fine places but soul killers inside

Caught up in bow ties, religious lies, and a piece of you just died

Love is most potent and lifts when nothing else can help

But to the knowledge at no direction college, had to introduce myself

Koi Nikole, M. A.

And dig into the trial and error scrolls, so many no one knows

To find real goals, I present to you this prose

One told me that we start hot and we grow cold

But their love starts cold and warms up while together growing old

And we don't know what the end should be to know the road to take

So we accept flicker and face glitter and stumble on the mask paint

But you know you can't build a future with one not prepared

And you know a bunch of feelings without a mission might leave you impaired

You know that love is a decision, honesty nourished, and builds trust

Maturity, commitment, responsibility, all that is a must

Can you quickly resolve conflict, does your actions raise the bar?

Do you make me want to be better, do you hold us in high regard?

Is our communication open and to our needs you're responsive?

Will I with you be safe, covered, stable, myself, and resilient?

Because short sightedness don't phase me but can you sustain

Our hearts, our home, our finances, our love forever remain

If you think you can, you will, if you think not, then that's that

I'm a life visionary, empire builder, and that's just where I'm at

The Phoenix Awakens

You Looking for Me?

I'm the sister in jeans, grocery shopping, and sports with my children

Cheering ladies, supporting family and friends in creative ventures

Sometimes people see bedroom eyes, & natural spun silk hair

Or even the thin waist that rides on the curves my hips bear

I'm more than my behind, my smile and my eyes

The wealth of knowledge and passion here will keep you so surprised

So I'm trying to say before you step to me

Be honest with yourself, 'Cuz I'm a Sag, be ready!

Be ready to embrace and enjoy life too

'Cuz I want nothing less and will give that to you

Ask, "what can I do to make sure she enjoys everything in life?

What's in her head and heart? Will she make a good wife?"

When I moved from the glare of the snare and set myself free

The dam broke! All over me

See I was in deprivation, starvation, dehydration

And my intimacy suffering from constipation

Can you believe all this love and intimacy I lacked?

Wait a minute ... Y'all I got my sexy back

Koi Nikole, M. A.

Did I portray sexy as physical or something you just see with your eyes

My sexiness is communion with uninhibited power and release in my mind

That made me resuscitate and remember who I was created to be

Great King can you keep this alive for me?

Then creativity power begins to swirl and move me

Like a tsunami in my soul, crash barricades that stilled me

That's why you can't step to me solely about my groove

'Cause you saw me sway the curves and my melanin so smooth

That was just a small piece I learned about my radiance

That cracked plaster in a shattered wall that imprisoned my highness

I'm an awakened female only a conscious male can see

All the multi facets of my jewels within me

I'd rather you marvel at my words than my curves

 To make sure you can reciprocate so I don't go in reverse

Blow my mind with your values and what you've achieved to par

Then speak to me gently and don't try to get too far

'Cuz we got time, digest my mind

Drip, drop me your essence with your actions and time

The Phoenix Awakens

You ain't looking for me if you can't give that little bit

And you really ain't looking for me if you chasing my slip

But if you're ready to elevate our consciousness & cup me in your Love

You might have been the man last night I was dreaming of

Are you Looking For Me?

Koi Nikole, M. A.

The Phoenix Awakens

Koi Nikole, M. A.

I Like The Way You Flow

I watch the butterfly flutter its wings and land

In my stomach, up my heart as I fold my hands

Thinking, oooh this feels nice like I'm on a cloud

All this silence but this soul is screaming loud

I don't really know what, what this feeling is

I would call it love but it feels so righteous

Kind of like Divine order has taken place

Because truth was brought forth so pain can be erased

How can a man make my mind, will, and intellect

Scream out and we ain't even together yet?

I think it was his words, his heart to give me understanding

Still, small, with wise truth, phileo for my yearning

To be right ... How is he doing this

I feel the transformational energy from my toes to my fingertips

And I just lay in this frequency feeling this powerful energy

Ain't no kind of lust, ain't none of that radiating from me

On Main Street passing the mic and ready to change

Steps, stepping up, sitting down, audience drawing in the flame

The Phoenix Awakens

If you can keep me right here and protect my heart the same

You may have found your forever love and I need no chains

Now I know I seem a little dramatic for what you think just happened

But it made me want to be the best me and all other pursuits abandon

Now that says a lot for some words not even relationally directed

Steady, low level intensity maybe my heart needed to be collected

But the one thing I know is that I want to feel that feeling some mo'

So can we meet again, I like the way you flow

Koi Nikole, M. A.

Hey New Girl

He loves to push my buttons and change my composure

He loves to feel like he has power over

The new girl is clueless and just sees my reaction

I was once her "everyone's-against-him" distracted

But I was his confidence to stand against others

And soon his wife drowning in his waters

It's a game we play, see he and I know

That it's a power struggle to restrict my flow

He fights for the position so desperately

Then enlist people with lies to put them against me

To make me feel outnumbered and unbelieved

It makes him feel better about himself, you see

I will not tit for tat because my mind is at ease

I will not think much on it because wisdom is in peace

I will think of mine and what I represent

And I'll brush that off without much resentment

But I am reminded of who I am dealing with

And know that my forces won't be reckoned with

I'll be mad with my head not my emotions

And walk away triumphant over this lil' commotion

Taking every other weekend for me

And raising my children like it's supposed to be

A new girl brings a new backbone, a new ally

The Phoenix Awakens

I can always tell the change, lil' devilment in the eyes
Obviously you miss me but miss me with that
NO you will not get a little purrrr from the cat

He purposely does anything that very well annoys me
Then he pulls you close, points, and says look she's crazy
I'm not jealous, petty, nor wanting the lack back
I'm just so far removed from that drama, I begin to attack
But I have to remember he does it for his audience
To create a picture for onlookers that have with me no experience
They don't know me from Eve just my reaction they see
They don't see the 100 times before he's reaching for me
So Hey new Girl, Look, I DON'T WANT YOUR MAN
Can you get him to stop wanting my energy, if you can?
Trying to forever diminish my radiance
That's why I had to get rid of this pestilence
So I must keep my heaven and lay these bricks
But with you here, I get less usual drama and benefits
So I just want to say Hey New Girl ... Thanks
For watching mine & motivating the bank
You are way better than me, I wouldn't get that far
To take him in your house and let him drive your car
So if you like it, I love it and blessings on your soul
As far as I'm concerned your work here is gold
Hey New Girl!

Koi Nikole, M. A.

"I have discovered in life
that there are ways of getting
almost anywhere you want to go,
if you really want to go. "
- *Langston Hughes*

The Phoenix Awakens

Equipping

Koi Nikole, M. A.

The Phoenix Awakens

I'm About To Equip You

I am not my history

But I arrested the smith so you can be a pistol see

You see, you better be glad my Daddy likes me to be a classy lady

Or I'd fill you full of holes with how they tried to play me

While sitting in pews telling me to do and my inner man says opposite

Than what my soul was crying through bars against the odds to stop it

So really my awakening came as my soul screamed out freedom from this hold

Answer from inside from the Most High, alignment being bestowed

So instead of this schizophrenia, they collided, merged and became one power

Who I was, am, and will be became one force now I am that fire

Happened in my heart so I can have the determination and momentum

To know when to accelerate, decelerate, or to swing it in neutral

And that push keeps my mind reaching, calculating, and strategizing the next step

So with fear put down, mind spinning my crown, my action is the only thing left

So as your sister please take my history and do what I did

Took all my fragments, put them together and build myself a bridge

Koi Nikole, M. A.

And understand every bridge was built by someone who first had no clue

But stepped out, even with doubt, and desired to do what they were destined to

But make sure you equip yourself with knowledge from the skilled and wise

Because one day someone will need your bridge or your shoes, your size

So know all that I've said about your heart, mind, and actions

Because time waits for no one and your victories are passing

But keep doing great things and stay on your supernatural high

There, nothing brings you down, they can't reach you in the sky

I'm about to equip you to fly

The Phoenix Awakens

They Thought

I had some strategic people unlike the rest

That must quiver whenever I do my best

But I never paid attention I was just being me

Outgoing, optimistic, intelligent, and free

I didn't understand why they just told so many lies

Or why for odd reasons my accomplishments they despised

They smoothed it over with nice words once again

So none of us would know what was really within

I could see but I thought nothing of it

By their actions from me something they covet

But they must feed distrust so that we don't try

And they must put up obstacles so we can't fly

They listen to your plans in disgust

Their response made you in you not trust

Feel less and question whatever you do

So you'll never have to confidence to hit the roof

Aaaah ... but when you get it

They gon' get it 'cuz they won't quit it

Koi Nikole, M. A.

Because when I focus on what I need to be healthy

Your words and actions still try to stab me

Spend a little time in my mind

Quiet the focus and pump up the shine

Get a vision and make those steps

Get a little bulk, get a little depth

Then I can see what they really see

And why their self-hatred has a hold on me

They know I could go, really go far

But they want me to stay where they are

Or under them whichever I allow them to do

See they make my dull look so true

But as you see

 I couldn't let that be

He say, she say, they say ooowweee

The only saying that really matters

Is from me!

The Phoenix Awakens

Koi Nikole, M. A.

When I Didn't Know Myself

When I thought all saints were saved, I was relationally inept
You were better off when I didn't know myself
Before I was able to step back from the situation
And see all the intricacies of this lil' incantation
One day, I was soaking the ambiance in a book store
I like to read titles up high and a little lower
Looked at this book a hypnotic magnetic attraction
Like I was reading stories out of my own crazy interactions
I just sat there in a daze I couldn't even move
So me, so real, so true, I walked those shoes
Blaming, denying, withholding, withdrawing
Punching walls, never home, gas lighting, & smirking
Dr. Jekyll, Mr. Hyde, overloading until emotionally feeble
Beg him to pay bills, help me, or prioritize for the children
Then my Wonder Woman kick in to make do perhaps
Thumbing my nose to get things done before I just collapse
Again ... And I didn't even choose to set me free
But your abandonment & desire to enjoy your life, actually freed me
Five perched as needy little baby birds
Momma gon' get it for you, you can believe those words

The Phoenix Awakens

But that journey made me work never to rely on anyone
Recognize liabilities and vampires, revolutionized in my belief system
Without people steering me back to the imprisoning path
Feeding my spirit solutions, discovering the strength I am
Growing and evolving as quiet as it was kept
You were better off when I didn't know myself

To know myself is not just knowing where my people come from
It is knowing the brilliance in me from when the world begun
Not just the resilience from bondage & hate others bring
But standing on a mound of rubble knowing I can strategize anything
To know ancestral principles working now and they produce life
And relying on others for self-knowledge won't suffice
But searching why don't these things ever really loose me
But cause oppression & perpetual enslavement to you see
A wise man said the world nor I could wait any later
You cannot spend your life he said in an infant incubator

Sometimes Most High has to kick you out and you're so confused
But you do know how to plug in, brush off, and get in tuned
And you cry like a newborn pushed through the birth canal
The air whips your skin, hurts your eyes, to cry is rationale
But you hear the familiar voice speaking like when you were inside
And it swaddles you close with love and less and less you cry
Then new faces come to assure you're perfect and it's okay
Did you know that most who are at this place are born this way?

Koi Nikole, M. A.

So I'm brand new, new world and a lot to do

And thank you so much, it's all because of YOU

Birthed to a new dimension, promoted, dark place left

You were better off when I didn't know myself

I'm a mother many times over, a leader above all things

I'm being born AND I'm swaddling, I can obviously do anything!!!!

The Phoenix Awakens

Unbothered

I made everyone's problems my problem

I made everyone's beliefs my problem

Grown men too blind to see, my problem

Fruit inspectin' women pressurin' me, my problem

Hater's expectations seem to be my problem

Carrying so much, about to hit rock bottom

Then I was spewed out of darkness into marvelous light

I could no more hear the screams that hindered my flight

As I lifted my head 'cuz I hit the ground hard

And pulled in my legs and checked for my heart

All I heard was screaming silence that echoes amid

But I could hear my heart beat & questions in my head

And there was so much I didn't know about me, so disjointed

Too many voices trying to control my life for what they wanted

And the more I rested in the place my mind collected

Infused what was mangled and the voices undetected

So every day I guard my essence and I remove all but me

Koi Nikole, M. A.

Because this is my life so let the Divine speak

I was created with certain kinds of gifts I do so well

They uplift, fuel my passion, and feed my broken inner self

Poised in my right mind fixed on a path to prosper

Staying true to self, no one else, remaining constantly unbothered.

The Phoenix Awakens

Positioning

Koi Nikole, M. A.

The Phoenix Awakens

Walk Away

I had to let it go because I hate how it feels

It hacks my body and my mind reels

The mind keeps repeating trying to find what could have changed

Keep bringing up the past that might have been the game

Trying to figure how I let it slip by

Thought everything was good, trying to figure why

It's a movie playing in my head all day long

The sinister words screaming loudly like a song

Now my countenance change and my body cringe

Now there's a rock in my stomach, it's caving in

I get up to walk and almost trip

Because the reeling moved to my legs and fingertips

My body feels so out of control

I can't hold it together, it's time to go

So I have to scream

STOP!

Koi Nikole, M. A.

You are the only you we have

And everything about you has to last

So it is imperative that you take control

So much to live for and so far to go

See you haven't seen the world through victory's eyes

When you're healthy and strong and flying high

Special times with family and new friends you love

Not missing a beat, soaring high above

Achieving things in your heart, your dreams

Experiencing what peace and love really means

So I had to let it go 'cuz I hate how it feels

It hacks my body and my mind reels

I had to say STOP and let it go

And give myself possibilities

My world would never know

I told myself ... Walk Away

The Phoenix Awakens

Get The Wheel

Found myself in a crazy place
Eventually I had to come face to face
And realize that my loyalty was displaced
When I realized it, the truth was all up in my face
See, I allowed a foreigner in
Not really knowing the heart within
The words were smooth and the grass looked green
But on the other side it was self-serving and mean
The more I did, the more they wanted
Like vampires, they sucked me dry & the real "me" stunted
I allowed it. Thought it was the way it was supposed to go
Abducted my essence time, potential, & trust though
See, I thought it was a coincidence
How when I asked questions, answers made no sense
But I kept a smile, giving all the while
Accepting what I could get, just enough to get by
I accepted it, opened my hand and took it
But because I thought the heart behind it wasn't crooked
So now I have to take the wheel and this is true
That wheel should have never even belonged to you
I had to realize others only know what I say
I needed the Most High Divine to equip me in my way
Where there's much pain and your heart yearns
Use your feelings, perception, and experience learned

Koi Nikole, M. A.

Who knows the ins and outs and how much it hurts
You know why you can't say THAT and the stabs that lurk
Let's uproot the blockage into a wise ear
To get it out of your heart and cleanse the wound with tears
Spill your broken heart with the emotions that won't stop stirring
So what do you need to do to stop this from reoccurring?
Get the wheel! Take it! Grab it! Yank the wheel!
Listen to the red flags your feelings yield
I thought I needed them then I asked myself WHY?
Cripple me, pull me down, and drain me dry
You jumped through the hoops, it goes no where
You say "They love me" knowing they really don't care
Wake up to Self-Love! Baby, 'cuz you all you got!
You made it! Though your battle scars might be a lot
I was once there in that same boat
But I kept it moving and don't even smell like smoke
Get the wheel!
You have everything to gain and so little to lose
It's such a big deal
Get the wheel

The Phoenix Awakens

Koi Nikole, M. A.

Take Time To Align

When the universe speaks do you listen?

Have you quieted voices, even yours, at your own volition?

Do you know what it means when snow melts and leaves part?

When the door closes but there's a burning purpose in your heart?

I can't see the future but I can see the wall's writing

Clues pointing, intuition uncovering, and love guiding

But you can't go unless you hear, so be quiet to take it in

Most High in you, with you, and is you, so let's begin

It is to live, let live, grow, love and be

One with the Divine that resides inside of me

I have to attend to riches or they're easily discarded

Until I understand what to do with it and its value guarded

I cannot create peace in my life until I learn what to do

And I cannot learn a thing without being a student to You

And I cannot learn how to quiet the voices and focus on this inception

To instruct our way, keep us safe, and rid all distractions

But I can take the mental ink, soul pen for the assignment

Because I am open for direction, knelt down, and in alignment

The Phoenix Awakens

Striving to live in balance that doors unceasingly open for me

To maintain the feeling on high being where I'm supposed to be

Just as Mary knelt at feet, digesting words for life

To steadily fuel the mission, life missiled to the next height

When the noise swirls, chaos verbs, mind spinning you just missed

Mouth, eyes, ears, body, all outlets occupied, no focus

So we must take the time to prune the vine of our mind

To take control of distractions that offset time after time

To begin with end in mind to get where you're going

To avoid the trap delusion of activity means your growing

Not just to reach higher but a higher calling to what matters most

Take the time to be assignment aligned and love your Innermost!

Koi Nikole, M. A.

Do it Time

Time is everything

You can miss the move of a lifetime by

2 minutes, 2 dollars, 2 incorrect answers

By messing with the ONE wrong person too long

Should have been erased and you just missed The One

So create a sense of urgency for the need for mastery

Because the experience might take years to make a recovery

You should be making it happen

In places, shaking hands, and scouting the land

Or creating the vision to be implemented because it's planned

Ready to launch the vision because it's planned

Today is the day to start because tomorrow is too late

To pave the road to the desired goal or it might never even go that way

So if you want to travel, a relationship, an A, or be a star, start right now

Because time waits for no one and all you need to know is how

How means what are the materials you need and go get your tools

Take the instructions, get started, and let your vision be your fuel

The Phoenix Awakens

Can't imagine where we'd be without the little vision we have

How life would drown us, overtake us, wouldn't have a chance

But every successful person has a moment of awakening

The pivotal moment the mind chooses to stop playing

And you really don't know how close you are to your dream

Faith and action opens doors, speed it up, and explode the whole thing

So it's not to blindly jump but pull it together and pursue

You've been hesitating and procrastinating but it's waiting for you

Make it possible

To starve your future is illogical

What time is it?! Do it time!

Koi Nikole, M. A.

The Phoenix Awakens

Rising

Koi Nikole, M. A.

I'm Back

Who you see today is not a new person

It is the healed emergence before my condition worsened

The smile, the glow, the wisdom, and the accomplishments

Were there before my life was interrupted by decadence

But they came to ransom my light like a covered coward

To bind me to their ownership and usurp all my power

It was so smooth, tickled my ears, and charming

Chivalrous and directed, not at all alarming

I remember grabbing at life to pull myself up

Spiritually, educationally, financially, new life construct

Shining my free spirit and zest for achieving

Then I was blinded by what I started believing

It took me years in a full circle to get back to me

Where the "Me" bound could finally be free

Yes, it hurt and yes, my rebound seemed unfair

That I would go through so much to finally get back here

Where I learn of the misconceptions and misdirection

To close my ears to really hear my ancestors discretion

The Phoenix Awakens

To build my innermost and remind me of my strength

To break shackles and lift my whole self by my chin

My heart had to break to make me awake

To the eroding journey I wouldn't forsake

Broke me to heal me and renewed my mindset

Open my eyes, even my third, realigned my higher self

Yes, I cried so much trying to find best for my family

But wiping my face because crying don't make money

Under foot crushing negativity, making them stepping stones

Because every wise person learns from things gone wrong

So now you are experiencing the butterfly from the chrysalis

I'm back in full swing

And my trajectory is limitless!!!

Koi Nikole, M. A.

I'm A Parachute

I feel like a parachute

Limitless and soaring beyond the view

But I'm attached to a boat only can go so far

Weighted down, parched, with no reservoir

As a matter of fact, BEAUTIFUL, with no ascent

More like a parachute driven with stakes like a tent

Have you ever seen a parachute pegged to the ground?

It's all the wrong dimensions, see parachutes are round

The vibrancy of splendor can't be adored

Hammered to the dirt, purpose ignored

The tent is good for shade and protection

But not for flying high in uncharted direction

But did I tell you ... I AM a parachute

Uh ... let me give you a little swoop

People marvel at me, at my artistry

For my ability to transcend beyond the weight of me

The way I am crafted rises high in the expanse

Given the right circumstance I more than have a chance

With a little heat and pressure, I still stay afloat

No steering wheel and no where but up to go

With the power of an ELEMENT you can't even SEE

Gives rise to my frame so gracefully

The Phoenix Awakens

So why in the world would I be content
To be pegged to the dirt like a tent
When my artistry is very clear to see
If I let them nail me down, it's all on me
So I'm opening my chute and I'm moving fast

Let the hot, radiating sun, free me at last

Koi Nikole, M. A.

The Phoenix Awakens

Koi Nikole, M. A.

Good Life

When you taste the sweet juices, succulent
Sun ripened, beautiful and loving it
As you feel the skin break and the juice drip on your skin
You gulp, wipe your mouth, and promise it will happen again
I think it exploded on my tongue and satisfied inside
As I leaned to the side and decided this angle to try
Have you ever bit into and had to pull away to see
Is this the same thing I was think' it would be
Yes ... it is
See when I picked you, I knew it would be a treat
A little taste of the unknown but good to eat
Should I choose this one or the one on the left?
Perfectly ripened ready, romantic eyes didn't help
Dreaming, creating in my mind the scene
Of what I wanted, this could change my way of thinking
And it did ...
Because when you disrobe to meet this new experience
You can't have anything weighing you 'cuz the juices are delicious
Did I tell you I taste, feel, and see it too
When you experience what I did, if you hesitate you a fool
So I'm not so easily moved at this point
Fixed on my gaze for that very moment

The Phoenix Awakens

The desire is not promiscuity but reaching that goal

To feel over and over that high ... that love glow

I apologize family did I blush

Just thinking ... about it gives me a rush

I want to rush out and make it mine

And scream "Family, I'm gon' grab at it this time!"

Can't let my past hold me back nor my failure

Can't listen to insecurities, fears, or self-made rumors

Can't accept people puttin' on me, obstructing my vision

Because they have none or for some other dumb reason

I have to get there, I want that taste again

Yes, its sweet juices tingling within

It's experiencing a life wanted but never knew

How good and necessary IT IS for you

So to all my friends & Fam who like where they're at

Know I love you but Queen Koi is going back

Because I don't want no more dry life

Running on a hamster wheel getting nowhere twice

Yes, I tasted it and loved and deserved it

I'm trying to put it into words that

I want that good life in every area see

I paid the cost, good karma, gonna get it for me

Not grabbing at straws and taken off drawers

But surprise gasps & breath takings that make you pause

Koi Nikole, M. A.

The good life and whatever that is for me and mine
To make us shake our heads and more respect the Divine
For this greatness I would not see
If I didn't reach the world outside of me
So when my feet hit the pavement, I'm gone
Whatever it takes to get me closer to my new home
Wiping this sweat and pulling my hair
Only concentration and grinding will get me there
And taste the good life in that back of my throat
I'm taking it all in, I want it! Take note!

Koi Nikole, M. A,

is a speaker, writer, training and development professional

who loves to write poetry.

She is the founder of Virtue Exchange,

whose mission is to enhance lives to the next life level

by getting unstuck and moving beyond.

She is a divorced, loving mother of the "Fabulous Five"

who work with her and cheer her on.

She is a proud graduate of Lindenwood University with a

BA in Corporate Communications and a

MA in Communications

with an emphasis in Training and Development.

She is not only very passionate about family and youth,

Koi is also an advocate for women and speaks in the community

about overcoming controlling behaviors and motivating people to move beyond their challenges to create a powerful life.

Koi Nikole, M. A.

The Phoenix Awakens ... Again!

Sharron Nicole, M. A.

www.ingramcontent.com/pod-product-compliance
Lightning Source LLC
Chambersburg PA
CBHW062059290426
44110CB00022B/2644